Rhapsody in Plain Yellow

Rhapsody in Plain Yellow

Marilyn Chin

W. W. Norton & Company New York London

"Love Song" by William Carlos Williams, from *Collected Poems: 1909–1939, Volume 1*, copyright by New Directions Publishing Corp. Reprinted by permission of New Directions Publishing Corp.

For information about permission to reproduce selections from this book, write to Permissions, W. W. Norton & Company, Inc., 500 Fifth Avenue, New York, NY 10110

The text of this book is composed in Centaur
Composition by Tom Ernst
Manufacturing by The Courier Companies, Inc.
Book design by Chris Welch
Production manager: Andrew Marasia

Library of Congress Cataloging-in-Publication Data

Chin, Marilyn.
Rhapsody in plain yellow / by Marilyn Chin.
p. cm.
ISBN 0-393-04167-0
1. Chinese American families—Poetry. 2. Mothers and daughters—Poetry. 3. Chinese Americans—Poetry. 4. Grandmothers—Poetry. I. Title.
PS3553.H48975 R48 2002
811'.54—dc21

2001044211

W. W. Norton & Company, Inc., 500 Fifth Avenue, New York, N.Y. 10110
www.wwnorton.com

W. W. Norton & Company Ltd., Castle House, 75/76 Wells Street, London WIT 3QT

2 3 4 5 6 7 8 9 0

for my mother, Wong Yuet Kuen, 1932–1994

and my grandmother, Fong Sui Lin, 1907–1996

Contents

Acknowledgments

I would like to thank the Corporation of Yaddo, the Blue Mountain Center, the Fulbright Foundation, the National Endowment for the Arts, Villa Montalvo, National Dong Hwa University in Taiwan and San Diego State University for their support. I would also like to thank the editors at the following publications, where the poems first appeared:

The American Voice   "Hospital in Oregon"

Brilliant Corners   "Emilies," "Hospital Interlude"

Field   "Family Restaurant," "Blues on Yellow (#2)"

The Iowa Review   "Get Rid of the X," "Summer Sonatina," "How Deep Is the River of God?" "I Am Waiting," "Libations," "Song of the Giant Calabash," "Variations on an Ancient Theme"

The Kenyon Review   "The Colonial Language Is English," "Cauldron"

Luna   "Identity Poem #99"

The Paris Review   "The True Story of Mortar and Pestle"

Parnassus   "Horse Horse Hyphen Hyphen," "Tonight while the Stars Are Shimmering"

The Progressive   "Blues on Yellow," "Hong Kong Fathersong," "Millennium, Six Songs," "So, You Fucked John Donne"

The Seattle Review   "To Pursue the Limitless"

Shenandoah   "Rhapsody in Plain Yellow"

Solo   "That Half Is Almost Gone"

Washington Square   "Horseyear"

ANTHOLOGIES

"The True Story of Mr. and Mrs. Wong," *Microfiction,* edited by Jerome
     Stern, W. W. Norton, 1996
"Cauldron," *The Best American Poetry, 1996,* edited by Adrienne Rich,
     Scribner, 1997
"That Half Is Almost Gone," *Pushcart Prize Anthology,* 1998
"Rhapsody in Plain Yellow," *Screaming Monkeys,* an anthology of Asian
     American Literature, edited by M. Galang, Coffee House
     Press, 2001
"Millennium, Six Songs," *Powerlines,* edited by Michael Warr, Tuchia
     Press, 1999

The stain of love
Is upon the world
Yellow, yellow, yellow

WILLIAM CARLOS WILLIAMS

Blues on Yellow

The canary died in the gold mine, her dreams got lost in the sieve.
The canary died in the gold mine, her dreams got lost in the sieve.
Her husband the crow killed under the railroad, the spokes hath shorn his wings.

Something's cookin' in Chin's kitchen, ten thousand yellow-bellied sapsuckers
  baked in a pie.
Something's cookin' in Chin's kitchen, ten thousand yellow-bellied sapsuckers
  baked in a pie.
Something's cookin in Chin's kitchen, die die yellow bird, die die.

O crack an egg on the griddle, yellow will ooze into white.
O crack an egg on the griddle, yellow will ooze into white.
Run, run, sweet little Puritan, yellow will ooze into white.

If you cut my yellow wrists, I'll teach my yellow toes to write.
If you cut my yellow wrists, I'll teach my yellow toes to write.
If you cut my yellow fists, I'll teach my yellow feet to fight.

Do not be afraid to perish, my mother, Buddha's compassion is nigh.
Do not be afraid to perish, my mother, our boat will sail tonight.
Your babies will reach the promised land, the stars will be their guide.

I am so mellow yellow, mellow yellow, Buddha sings in my veins.
I am so mellow yellow, mellow yellow, Buddha sings in my veins.
O take me to the land of the unreborn, there's no life on earth without pain.

Rhapsody in Plain Yellow

That Half Is Almost Gone

That half is almost gone,
>   the Chinese half,
the fair side of a peach,
>   darkened by the knife of time,
fades like a cruel sun.

In my thirtieth year
>   I wrote a letter to my mother.

I had forgotten the character
>   for "love." I remember vaguely
the radical "heart."
>   The ancestors won't fail to remind you

the vital and vestigial organs
>   where the emotions come from.

>   But the rest is fading.
>   A slash dissects in midair,
ai, ai, ai, ai,
>   more of a cry than a sigh

(and no help from the phoneticist).

You are a Chinese!

        My mother was adamant.

You *are* a Chinese?

        My mother less convinced.

Are you *not* Chinese?

        My mother now accepting.

As a cataract clouds her vision,

        and her third daughter marries
a Protestant West Virginian

        who is "very handsome and very kind."

The mystery is still unsolved—

        the landscape looms

over man. And the gaffer-hatted fishmonger—

        sings to his cormorant.

And the maiden behind the curtain

                    is somebody's courtesan.

Or, merely Rose Wong's aging daughter

          Pondering the blue void.

You are a Chinese—said my mother
                    who once walked the fields of her dead—

Today, on the 36th anniversary of my birth,

I have problems now
                    even with the salutation.

The Colonial Language Is English

Heaven manifests its duality
My consciousness on earth is twofold
My parents speak with two tongues
My mother's tongue is Toisan
My father's tongue is Cantonese
The colonial language is English
I and thou, she and thee
My mother is of two minds
The village and the family
My mother loves me, I am certain
She moulded my happiness in her womb
My mother loves my brother, certainly
His death was not an enigma
Yet, it, too, had its mystery

I had willed it in my heart
I had condemned him in his crib
When I touched his round, Buddha face
Drank in his soft, infant beauty
Cain and Abel had a sister
Her name is Tiny Pearl
Too precious to be included in their story
Her small throat trilled in vain

The Tao of which we speak is not the eternal Tao
The name that we utter is not the eternal name
My mother is me, my father is thee
As we drown in the seepage of Sutter Mill

Take a Left at the Waters of Samsara

There is a bog of sacred water
    Behind a hedgerow of wild madder
Near the grave of my good mother
    Tin cans blossom there

The rust shimmers like amber
    A diorama of green gnats
Ecstatic in their veil dance
    A nation of frogs regale

Swell-throated, bass-toned
    One belts and rages, the others follow
They fuck blissfully
    Trapped in their cycle

Of rebirth, transient love
    Unprepared for higher ground
And I, my mother's aging girl
    Myopic, goat-footed

Got snagged on an unmarked trail
    The road diverged; I took
The one less traveled
    Blah, blah

I sit at her grave for hours
    A slow drizzle purifies my flesh
I still yearn for her womb
    And can't detach

I chant new poems, my best fascicle
    Stupid pupil, the truth
Is an oxymoron and exact
    Eternity can't be proven to the dead

What is the void but motherlessness?
    The song bellies up
The sun taketh
    The rain ceases to bless

Chinese Quatrains (The Woman in Tomb 44)

The aeroplane is shaped like a bird
Or a giant mechanical penis
My father escorts my mother
From girlhood to unhappiness

A dragonfly has iridescent wings
Shorn, it's a lowly pismire
Plucked of arms and legs
A throbbing red pepperpod

Baby, she's a girl
Pinkly propped as a doll
Baby, she's a pearl
An ulcer in the oyster of God

Cry little baby clam cry
The steam has opened your eyes
Your secret darkly hidden
The razor is sharpening the knife

Abandoned taro-leaf boat
Its lonely black sail broken
The corpses are fat and bejeweled
The hull is thoroughly rotten

The worm has entered the ear
And out the nose of my father
Cleaned the pelvis of my mother
And ringed around her fingerbone

One child beats a bedpan
One beats a fishhook out of wire
One beats his half sister on the head
Oh, teach us to fish and love

Don't say her boudoir is too narrow
She could sleep but in one cold bed
Don't say you own many horses
We escaped on her skinny mare's back

Man is good said Meng-Tzu
We must cultivate their natures
Man is evil said Hsun-Tzu
There's a worm in the human heart

He gleaned a beaded purse from Hong Kong
He procured an oval fan from Taiwan
She married him for a green card
He abandoned her for a blonde

My grandmother is calling her goslings
My mother is summoning her hens
The sun has vanished into the ocean
The moon has drowned in the fen

Discs of jade for her eyelids
A lozenge of pearl for her throat
Lapis and kudzu in her nostrils
They will rob her again and again

Emilies: Aria for My Mother

(SHATTERED SONNETS, SERIES 1–3)

My soul upon a messy Eucalyptus

a condor's eye view

(she, too, a dying species)

I am propped horizontal

hands on chest

white silk blouse to throat

Rouge: blue unguent

pink matte

a bullet of passion

I wear as an amulet

a centimeter from my heart

Amazing Grace Yeah amazing!

no questioning of whose God

Which dharma? Whose stupa?

The requiem is a freeway's susurrus

a tap/tapping of the nails

Signed

sealed

delivered

I'm yours

trill Stevie's blind hymnal

into the

                    Digger's   Distant   Earphones
O the blue consciouness of ox
                         His flanks bleared from my gaze
(he doesn't have a pension)
                    Nor
                         should I give a damn now
O the sky and the science of wilting
                              asters   chrysanthemum   gladiolas
ecstatic colors
               white blight   bright purple
                                   Bled Dyed
in Suzuki's giant hothouse
                    the lapels the wrists the ardor
just a shredded hindrance
                    More to sweep away
Illumination
          is death's eldest daughter
                              False Modesty   I bloomed too late
My poesies   My liturgies   My mantras
                         My clay tablets   My dull writ
1776 ditties
               in a faux cherry ossuary
Me and silence
                    and some strange race   WRECKED!

The Great Mother manifests

                    The Great Mother hidden

All ye all ye all sent free!

                  One shaft of white light

then another

           another

                O minions and

thralldoms

         O the great pomp of living and dying

                        The secret of the fly whisk

is the fly

           wringing   wringing his hands

the fat one fondling my ears

                the thin one measuring my head

O holy   holy choir

            the living Baching with the dead

first sassed Billie

          then Janice

               now Aretha *murrrrmurrrs*

the sticky   wicky   icky

                ko-ans

                    of love

Millennium, Six Songs

I.

Black swollen fruit dangling on a limb
Red forgotten flesh sprayed across the prairie
Parched brown vines creeping over the wall
Yellow winged pollen, invisible enemies

Boluses without homesteads, grubs without a voice
Burrowed deeply into this land's dark, dark heart
Someday, our pods and pupae shall turn in the earth
And burgeon into our motherlode's bold beauty

II.

We're a seed on the manure, on the sole of your shoe
We're the louse trapped in your hank of golden hair
We're the sliver that haunts beneath your thumbnail
We're the church mouse you scorched with a match but lived

We're the package wrapped, return address unknown
We're the arm lowered again, again, a bloodied reverie
We've arrived shoeless, crutchless, tousle-haired, swollen-bellied
We shall inherit this earth's meek glory, as foretold

III. (FOR LEAH, MY NIECE)

They gave you a title, but you were too proud to wear it
They gave you the *paterland*, but you were too lazy to farm it

Your condo is leaking, but you're too angry to repair it
Your dress has moth holes, but you're too sentimental to toss it

You're too bored to play the lute, it hangs on the wall like an ornament
The piano bites you, it's an eight-legged unfaithful dog

Love grows in the garden, but you're too impudent to tend it
A nice Hakka boy from Ogden, so hardworking, so kind

The prayer mat is for prayer, not for catamite nipple-piercing
The Goddess wags her finger at your beautiful wasteland

A dream deferred, well, is a dream deferred

IV. (Janie's retort, on her fortieth birthday)

The same stars come around and around and around
The same sun peeks her head at the horizon
The same housing tract, the same shopping center
The same blunt haircut: Chinese, Parisian, Babylonian
The same lipstick: red and it comes off on your coffeecup
The same stars come around and around and around
The same sun tarries in the late noon sky
The same word for mom: *Ah ma, madre, mere, majka*
The same birthbabe: bald, purplish, you slap to make cry
The same stench: mother's milk, shit and vomit
The same argument between a man and a woman
The same dog, hit by a car, the same escaped canary
The same turkey for Thanksgiving, Christmas and the New Year
The same three-tiered freeway: Istanbul, Tokyo, San Diego
The same hill, the same shanty town, the same lean-to
The same skyscraper: Hong Kong, Singapore, Toledo
The same soup: chicken, though the veggies may vary
The same rice for supper: white, brown or wild
The same stars come around and around and around
The same sun dips her head into the ocean
The same tree in the same poem by the same poet
The same old husband: saggy breasts, baggy thighs
The same blackness whether we sleep or die

V.

Whoever abandoned her grandmother at the bus stop
Whoever ran in and out the door like a blind wind
   spinning the upside-down prosperity sign right side up again
Whoever lost her virtue   in darkly paneled rooms   with white boys
Whoever prayed for round eyes
  and taped her eyelids in waiting
Whoever wore platform shoes
  blustering taller than her own kind
Whoever sold her yellow gold for Jehovah
Whoever discarded her jade Buddha for Christ

VI.

Why are you proud, father, entombed with the other woman?
Why are you proud, mother, knitting my shroud in heaven?
Why are you proud, fish, you feed the greedy mourners?
Why are you proud, peonies, your heads are bowed and weighty?
Why are you proud, millennium, the dialect will die with you?
Why are you proud, psalm, hammering yourself into light?

Cauldron

General Yuan Shih Kai
your horse went mad.
He danced a ribbon
around the character for "chaos."
And oh, such a character
it was.
Oh grand master,
won't you let the light in.
This human destiny,
scroll and colophon,
painterly and evocative—
is the greatest masterpiece,
dark as it is.
There are horses and chariots,
Chin's terracotta soldiers,
vengeful pale ghosts.
The men—chivalrous and virile
behind forged armors.
The women—forebearers of sorrow
in soft cloud chignons.
The cauldron is heavy—
our bones will flavor the pottage,
our wrists will bear its signature.
As the kingdom's saga trills on,
familial and personal,

the great panorama of Loyang
blusters in its silent gallows
and the war-torn vermilion glow
of eternal summer.
There is my granduncle
plotting to sell my mother
for a finger of opium.
There is my grandmother
running after him, tottering
down the grassy knolls
in her bound feet
and unraveled hair.
Her cry would startle the ages.
Meanwhile, the chrysanthemum blooms
shamelessly, beautifully,
confident of a fast resolve.
Yes, all would fructify notwithstanding—
all which is beautiful must bloom,
all which blooms is beautiful.
My grandmother's cry would chill the gorges,
remembered by the caretaker of pines
in the Shaolin monastery
and the young boy taking the tonsure,
remembered by the blind sage Vitapithaca,
his acolyte the King Monkey,

the Sandman and the pusillanimous pig,
remembered by the Emperor of Heaven
and the Yellow Prince of Hell.
O Goddess of Mercy, why have you been remiss?
I have burnt joss sticks at your ivory feet.
I have kept the sanctity of my body
and the cleanliness of mind.
I have washed my heart of bad intentions.
And she hobbles, down past the oatgrass,
past the hollyhocks and persimmons,
orange and fragrant in their wake,
past the buffalo trough, past her lover,
whom she would not name,
past the priest and his valley of carillon,
and the red, red sorghum of her childhood.
Past the oxen and her family ox
in a rare moment without his yoke,
past the girls chattering behind the sassafrass,
and the women bathing and threshing hemp.
Past the gaffer-hatted fisherman
and his song of the cormorant.
Oh shoulder thy burdens, old cudgel, shoulder them
in your brief moments of reprieve and splendor.
My grandmother ran, driven by the wind.
The pain in her hooves, those tender hooves,

those painful lotuses could not deter her.
As the warlord's bamboo whip flailed
over the unyielding sky,
and the Japanese bayonets flash
against the ancient banyans,
all history would step aside, grant her passage.

What is destiny, but an angry wind—plagues and salvages,
death knocking on your neighbor's door, and you dare look out
your window, relieved that you were spared for another hour.

So gather your thoughts, brief butterfly, your water clock dries.
Shallow river, shallow river, how shall I cross?

Footsteps so light, the fallow deer can't hear her.
Heart so heavy, the village women would sink a stone
in her name each time they crossed the shoals.
The soothsayer in the watchtower espies her.
O destiny-in-a-whirlwind, serpent-in-the-grass,
she inches toward her ailing half brother.
Dragging feudalism's gangrene legs;
their kind is wan and dying.
The child on his back, limp with exhaustion,
answers to my grandmother's call.

Night will lower its black knife,
only the lantern will bear witness now.
The bridge is crossed. My mother is saved.
Her hemp doll dragged downstream by the river.

Broken Chord Sequence

ALTAR (#3)

Why cry over dried flowers?
They're meant to be straw.
Why cry over miniature roses?
They're meant to be small.

Why cry over Buddha's hand citron?
Why cry over the hidden flower?
Why cry over Mother's burnt forehead?
Her votive deathglow, her finest hour.

Hospital Interlude

I rented a red Miata   I returned to the hospital
I returned to the hospital   and climbed the wall
I climbed the wall   through a dim-lit corridor
The dim-lit corridor   leads to her empty sickroom
Her sickroom was empty   but the moon was full
The moon was full   the cicadas were crying
The cicadas were crying   *her unmade bed in the moonlight*
Her unmade bed in the moonlight   *an eternal stain*

I veered and turned   but couldn't find the exit
I couldn't find the exit   I said to my mother
I said to my mother   *the song is not over*
The song is not over   *you forgot to tutor me*
You forgot to tutor me   *the last secret phrases*
The last secret phrases   in my rented red Miata
In my rented red Miata   I veered and turned
I veered and turned   but couldn't find the exit

I couldn't find the exit   *the // rain // in // my // hair*

Hospital in Oregon

Shhh, my grandmother is sleeping,
They doped her up with morphine for her last hours.
Her eyes are black and vacant like a deer's.
She says she hears my grandfather calling.

A deerfly enters through a tear in the screen,
Must've escaped from those there sickly Douglas firs.
Flits from ankle to elbow, then lands on her ear.
Together, they listen to the ancient valley.

Song of the Giant Calabash

At the market I bought a calabash
    to make my father stew.
He spat and called it bitter,
    his sputum seeded the ground.

Out came a giant calabash
    shaped like Buddha's long head.
I baked it with honey and jujubes
    to feed my father again.

"Useless girl! I said I hate calabash."
    He slapped his bowl to the floor.
The rains poured down from heaven,
    green mists and healing clouds blue.

Again another calabash
    rounder than Buddha's mighty torso.
I mixed it with wild cat and agar
    and called it "A Monk's Mock Lamb."

"Dead girl! I said I hate calabash,"
    he burst into a thousand flames.
His head smashed opened—well, like a calabash.
    He perished, headlong into his bowl.

Faint light into a silent altar.
  Blue, blue the mist of spring.
The sun shone through her hardy trellis
  and danced on his empty bed.

This morning I cut my last calabash,
  carved a large bottle-gourd of dreams.
I shall float her down the river
  into Buddha's eternal dawn.

Hong Kong Fathersong

I followed you up Victoria Peak
    where you kissed a German visitor.
Then you took her to the Furama Hotel
    and bought her a drink with an umbrella.
I followed you into the Red Orchid Room
    and pulled your skinny body off of her.
Then you rode that hydrofoil to Macau
    shaking your fist at heaven,
lost ten Hong Kong thousand in Pai-gow,
    Happy Valley's your next exit.

You prowled on Cat Street into dawn.
    A "Luverly" in Mandarin dress kicked you,
"Can't buy something with nothing, Chinaman,
    haven't you learned your lesson?"
I dragged you back to Granny's Wanchai flat
    where Mother's pregnant with Sister.
"I won't tell the Uncles that you've been bad
    if you pay me a hundred dollars.
A hundred *American* dollars, dear Father,
    a hundred *American* dollars."

Get Rid of the X

My shadow followed me to San Diego
  silently, she never complained.
No green card, no identity pass,
  she is wedded to my fate.

The moon is a drunk and anorectic,
  constantly reeling, changing weight.
My shadow dances grotesquely,
  resentful she can't leave me.

The moon mourns his unwritten novels,
  cries naked into the trees and fades.
Tomorrow, he'll return to beat me
  blue—again, again and again.

Goodbye Moon, goodbye Shadow.
  My husband, my lover, I'm late.
The sun will plunge through the window.
  I must make my leap of faith.

How Deep Is the River of God?

How deep is the river of God? They'll throw us in to drown.
How deep is our love for Mother? The river not deep enough.

Poetry is a vast orphanage, in which you and I are stars.
One robe, one bowl, silent pilgrimage, the river filled with martyrs.

Look for us, look for us, Mister Coyote, thirsting for our thighs and
    fingerbones,
Wait for us, wait for us, Brethren Condor, to clean the sleep from our
    eyes.

Guan guan cry the golden ospreys, in the borderlands we cry.
Our little eggs, little eggs grow into big ospreys

To lay little eggs again, *guan guan.*
Our miasma will ooze through the suburbs and gobble up their minds.

I Am Waiting

I am waiting for my transformation
Breasts to grow fuller, lips to turn bolder
Myopia to clear
Eyelids to fold over

I am waiting for the #26 bus
Between Grant and California
One arrives, filled with noisy Chinese people
So, I wait for another

I am waiting for my prince on a white, white steed
I am waiting for the Fall
The Fall of Falls
A sleepless September

I am waiting for love, the love of all loves
I am waiting for my Lord
I am waiting to unlearn ecstasy
For the cloaca of utopia to gallop over us

I am waiting for the dead to reawaken
How beautiful her sleep, how beautiful

LIBATIONS, SONG 10

Have you filled the cups for libations, my sister?
No, I have no wine, no hen to offer, my brother.

Are there fresh peonies in the altar, my sister?
No, winter is cruel and the petals have fallen, my brother.

Did you cord my hat, patch my jacket, my sister?
No, I have no cord nor rags for mending, my brother.

Did you catch a carp from the river, my sister, and reserved me the head?
No, the river is dry, my brother, where the dead must leave their faces.

Did you marry my friend, the kerosene merchant, my sister? Did he
    warm your bed?
Yes, I married your friend the kerosene merchant, by twilight
    our flame was gone.

Why is the cauldron empty, my sister, and no fire to warm the stew?
If there's no kindling for the living, my brother, would there be flesh
    for the dead?

Variations on an Ancient Theme: The Drunken Husband

The dog is barking at the door
"Daddy crashed the car"
"Hush, kids, go to your room
Don't come out until it's over"
He stumbles up the dim-lit stairs
Drops his Levi's to his ankles
"Touch me and I'll kill you," she says
Pointing a revolver at his head

The dog is barking at the door
She doesn't recognize the master
She sniffs his guilty crotch
Positioned to bite it off
"Jesus, control your dog
A man can't come back to his castle"
"Kill him, Ling, Ling," she sobs
Curlers bobbing on her shoulders

The dog is barking at the door
"Quiet, Spot, let's not wake her"
The bourbon is sour on his breath
Lipstick on his proverbial collar
He turns on the computer in the den
He calms the dog with a bone
Upstairs she sleeps, facing the wall
Dreaming about the Perfume River

The dog is barking at the door
He stumbles in swinging
"Where is my gook-of-a-wife
Where are my half-breed monsters?"
There is silence up the cold stairs
No movement, no answer
The drawers are open like graves
The closets agape to the rafters

The dog is barking at the door
He stumbles in singing
"How is my teenage bride?
How is my mail-order darling?
Perhaps she's pretending to be asleep
Waiting for her man's hard cock"
He enters her from behind
Her sobbing does not deter him

The dog is barking at the door
What does the proud beast know?
Who is both Master and intruder?
Whose bloody handprint on the wall?
Whose revolver in the dishwater?
The neighbors won't heed her alarm
She keeps barking, barking
Bent on saving their kind

Bold Beauty

She opened her eyes and he was already within her,
though the lore said that a mere kiss would suffice.
The song distorted on the tongue of the soothsayer—
no need to struggle, he would take her away
on his white, white steed and panniers of riches.
In veils and swathing she would be reborn as queen.

Out in the ramparts the last village seared.
Her parents cried out for their lost girlchild,
"Ts'ai Yen, Ts'ai Yen," but the sky did not answer.
Her thin jade bracelet shattered into five dazzling pieces,
one for each element that made up the stars.
A constellation of black hair was her last missive.

In antechamber and darkness she feels him again.
The tale is the rapture of the water clock, pain
which burns into pleasure, burns into the hours.
Our heroine turns over and slits the throat of her beloved.
She would avenge her family, her sovereignty, her dead.
She who survives to tell the tale shall hold the power.

The True Story of Mortar and Pestle

for my sister, Jane

Nobody understood her cruelty to herself. In this life, cruelty begets cruelty, and before long, one would have to chop off one's own hand to end the source of self-torture. Yet, we continue, Sister Mortar pounding on Sister Pestle. The hand refuses to retreat, as if to retreat would mean less meat on the table.

She, Mortar, the presentable one: clean, well-kept, jade cross, white colonial pinafore, shiny knees and elbows, straight As, responsible hall monitor, future councilwoman. She is Yang: heaven, sunlight, vigorous, masculine, penetrator, the monad.

She, Pestle: disheveled, morose, soft-spoken, a fearful dark crucible. She is Yin: heaven's antithesis, moony, fecund, feminine, absorption, the duad.

The outer child had everything to live for: tenure, partnership in the firm, shapely breasts, strong legs, praise from a few key critics, the love of a good man.

The inner child was denied food, yet food was ample. She was denied sleep, yet darkness descended as day.

Justice was the hateful stepfather. His voice was loud, truculent in their ear, *If you succeed there would be no applause; if you fail, there, too, would be silent reckoning.*

Listen to that serious pounding of the ages . . . not nocturnal lovemaking of the muses, but the bad sister pounding the good. Somewhere in the scintillating powder we grind into light.

The True Story of Mr. and Mrs. Wong

Mrs. Wong bore Mr. Wong four children, all girls.
One after the other, they dropped out like purple plums.
One night after long hours at the restaurant and a bad gambling bout
Mr. Wong came home drunk. He kicked the bedstead and shouted,
"What do you get from a turtle's rotten womb but rotten turtle eggs?"
So, in the next two years he quickly married three girls off to a missionary,
a shell-shocked ex-Marine and an anthropologist. The youngest ran away
to Hollywood and became a successful sound specialist.

Mr. Wong said to Mrs. Wong, "Look what happened to my progeny.
My ancestors in heaven are ashamed. I am a rich man now. All the
Chinese restaurants in San Jose are named Wong. Yet, you couldn't offer
me a healthy son. I must change my fate, buy myself a new woman. She
must have fresh eggs, white and strong." So, Mr. Wong divorced Mrs.
Wong, gave her a meagre settlement and sent her back to Hong Kong,
where she lived to a ripe old age as the city's corpse beautician.

Two years ago, Mr. Wong became a born-again Christian. He now loves
his new wife, whose name is Mrs. Fuller-Wong. At first she couldn't
conceive. Then, the Good Lord performed a miracle and removed three
large polyps from her womb. She bore Mr. Wong three healthy sons
and they all became corporate tax accountants.

The Cock's Wife

In the end of the millennium, the cock is still beautiful.
He crows in the morning in his magnificent red beard.
But the cock's wife was shorn of her dazzling pink overcoat,
To be bathed in sea salt, laid bare for the imperial table.
Head held high, she feigned ignorance of her own demise.
Her tiny yellow fluffies touched wingspans, vowed to avenge her.
They expounded on dialectical points, lollygaged at The Hague,
Scratched and squawked, pecked at ankles,
but stood silent as the masses devoured her.
Aghast, they fled for their lives,
Then paraphrased her in a fable.

Where We Live Now (Vol. 3, #4)

eternal noonscape

I don't love you for your savage beauty
not for your pale fragrant flesh,
not for your sun-spectred countenance
and your stars that paralyze the sky,
not for your silver-timbred limbs scarred
by a thousand axes. I yearn for
all you can give me, the wild geese
that wing over the moon blindly.
The white egret on a dunghill stands
on ceremony, on one thin leg,
calling her mate: hello, hello,
we have had a bad connection
since Ma Bell shattered—
cicadas chivvy in the rosemary,
blue jays wreak havoc
on the wires—the frogs in the pond
mock the ocean and its depth:
they cannot know their limitations.
Jacarandas wave their purple dare.
Lush lantana cannot hide
the local banal geckos; the sun sets
on the frontier Korean grass;
at the Aztec watering hole
horses, motorcycles, dump trucks neigh
to the moon; paisley, dizzy succulents,

slipshod hillside robes
expose gray, bruised thighs of the barrio;
large blooms of oleander, star jasmine;
scentless forsythia brilliant yellow.
Vacuous verbena, red hibiscus dance around
the Great Mother's wide helm,
mouthing the earth's gaping hollows.

———————

A jumbo jet careens between sun and moon—
a small man controls her destiny,
veers into the vast blue loneliness.
Hello, hello, won't you call me from San Francisco,
Tel Aviv, Hong Kong, Canton, Ohio,
from your corporate e-mail address,
from your turbid moods and peccadilloes?
Won't you ring me from the netherside
of the universe, from the back entry
of Eido, . . . where the moonscape appears friendly
and truth is not a liability.
Home is the grandest illusion: Papa's
failed restaurants, Mama's broken wren
of a neck in the nest's warm alcove.
Will the thundering bring new rain?
Will I rise again and again

to greet the sun's bright welcome?
Or will it be another sleepless night
of Prozac and Yo-Yo Ma's morbiferous cello?
Alone, within you, without you,
in the Southern California morass—
arrogance, ignorance, indifference,
wave after wave the clean hubbub of freeway
delivering me, delivering me
from nowhere to nowhere, the landscape
murmuring between waking and slumber.
Lover, I am calling you
from the southernmost hinterlands,
I am scrawling a long love plume
mocking my own befuddlement.
Crows and wood doves loiter,
orange proroguing trumpet flowers
irradiated and gargantuan,
loose liana creeping up the rectum of a wall.
Hummingbirds drink
from my sanguinary confections
(preferring fiction over truth)
in plastic, vulval-red flowers.
O how their small bodies suspend,
a brilliant trapeze of the soul.
O my little winging bee-bird,

O my beauteous formula,
O Bird, O Bard—how I object
to this feeble corollary!
As you sip this perfect concoction
from my inner brown thigh,
perhaps the creatures will make peace
with these human contusions.
Perhaps Art doesn't matter—
only happiness, an eternal noonscape
more substance than shadow.
Your limp arm draped over my pillow,
the morning sun kissing it so.

———————

O let the bees make honey from an iron sleeve,
let the grille beneath the house
be their sanctuary. But the wasps
that bear no honey, I have scheduled
Tuesday for their extermination.
Hello, hello, yo! Baby, Odysseus!
Will you return from your ten-year exile?
Could you love me again
in our quiet domesticity?
Penelope Wong's been waiting with her sad kohl eyes.
Could we mend the fissures in the bowl?

Meanwhile, the ocean roars against the shoals,
twenty miles of La Jolla where
the rich whites live; where sandpipers dance,
their tiny, skittery legs
foraging, pecking, never ceasing.
Another hateful colleague, another disturbing ritual
defines me—that static calamity
spreading from home to divorced home,
welling up, attempting to break
my contemplation:
                    my skinhead neighbor says
that he believes in segregation,
in racial purity, *HITLER ELIMINATED THE JEWS*
FOR REASONS OF OVERPOPULATION—IT WAS
BEFORE THE PILL, HA-HA . . . IN 1955,
WEBSTER'S NEW WORLD DICTIONARY *CITES 'A RACIST'*
AS "ONE WHO IS PROUD OF ONE'S RACE."
The devil is bronze and he, too, is the flesh of God.
He went on, that little fatherfucker,
blondly in his monster truck,
that barbarian drone, that hard-metal music.
Once, I paid him fifty dollars
for pruning my exuberant loquats;
the muse, extravagant by nature,
self-appointed enigma,

Minister Plenipotentiary to the Holy See,
with her ambiguous smile and silent condescension,
deigns to immortalize him here.

————

It may be plausible to assert that
phenomena have explanations,
or in laymen's terms,
they have causes.
In the picture window I yell,
Move it, El Grosso, move it.
He thinks I am saying,
Hello, lover, hello.

Zenfully, zenfully,
he drove northward, gun rack
rattling through blue void.

> *Zenfully, northward*
> *gun rack rattling*
> *blue void*

zenfully

gunrack   rattling

blue void

gun rack

blue

void

When my mother painted bamboo
         She saw bamboo and not herself.
Gladly, she left her body.
         Her body hardened into bamboo.
A fresh breeze made her sing;
         And she stood, singing,
One with the forest.

When / my / mother / painted / bamboo /

She / saw / bamboo / and / not / herself /

Gladly / she / left / her / body /

Her / body / hardened / into / bamboo /

A / fresh / breeze / made / her / sing /

And / she / stood / singing/

One / with / the / forest /

Hello, hello,
You had better listen to your moral thoughts,
Ms. Lookeast, Ms. Lookeast,
your mother is the right hand of Buddha,
you're more like the left hand of darkness,
snot-nosed, tousle-haired;
a persistent 5 o'clock shadow's
not very comely on a Chinese American woman.
In deep drought, knowledge does not hold water.
I'm slothful, sleepy,
no energy to divert the rivers.
The palm tree shreds a mess near my boudoir.
The rats make remorseful love in the sheaves.
The local flora's invaded by exotic seedlings;
cacti mixed with imperial cherries, mixed
with woodsy wildflowers, mixed
with cheap bareroot roses from "Home Depot."

———————

A Chink has moved into their neighborhood
and there's nothing they can do about it.

A hawk tarries, and the wind chimes call
infrequently: this exile, this malaise,
this complacency. In this motherless desert heat
I am missing you. Welcome, sweet sojourner,
welcome to Chin's promontory.
No giant statue of Buddha or gilded pagoda
carved in mist; no Mao's Yenan caves
deep in the rhapsody of revolution.
No majestic Gueilin, no silk route to enlightenment,
no "Red Detachment of Women"—jaded scabbards, piqued bayonets,
pirouette, arabesque, changez, changez into the distance—
but a view of the freeway and the borderlands:
California's best kept secret. You said,
Your ass, your beautiful ass fascinates me.
So, the birds chirp *ming ming,*
and the dogs bark *hung hung.*
A ginkgo traveled ten thousand miles from her homeland
to become a weed tree in the new kingdom,
and another blight cracks through the groundswell.
I wear a watch to bed to remind myself
of my own dying. I nail a calendar on the wall
so that each day shall pass in vain.

Come back, come back, my soul, I summon you,
come back to San Diego. The sun's so hot
we can fry an egg on the blacktop
and make soap with the lye.

Blues on Yellow (#2)
for Charles

Twilight casts a blue pall on the green grass
    The moon hangs herself on the sickly date palm near the garage

Song birds assault a bare jacaranda, then boogy toward Arizona
    They are fewer this year than last

Sadness makes you haggard and me fat
    Last night you bolted the refrigerator shut

X-tra, X-tra, read all about it
    Chinese girl eats herself to death

Kiss a cold banquet and purge the rest
    There's room in the sarcophagus if you want it

I keep my hair up in a bereavement knot
    Yours grow thinner, whiter, a pink skullcap

My Levi's hang loosely and unzipped
    You won't wash, won't shave or dress

I am your rib, your apple, your adder
    You are my father, my confessor, my ox, my draft

Heartbreak comes, again, when does it come?
　When your lamp is half dim and my moon is half dark

Horse Horse Hyphen Hyphen
Border Ghazals

I.

I hate, I love, I don't know how
I'm biracial, I'm torn in two

Tonight, he will lock me in fear
In the metal detector of love

Rapeflowers, rapeseeds, rapiers
A soldier's wry offerings

He will press his tongue
Into my neighing throat

I can speak three dialects badly
I want you now behind the blue door

In a slow hovercraft of dreams
I saw Nanking from a bilge

Some ashes fell on his lap
I'm afraid it's my mother

The protocol is never to mention her
While we are fucking

II.

The bad conceit, the bad conceit police will arrest you
Twin compasses, twin compasses cannot come

Your father is not a car, not a compass and not God
Though he vanished in his sky-blue convertible Galaxy with a blonde

He kept crawling back to us, back to us
Each time with a fresh foot mangled

One emperor was named Lickety, the other named Split
Suddenly, the soup of chaos makes sense

Refugees roaming from tent to tent to tent, looking for love
The banknote is a half note, an octave above God

O the great conjugator of curses: shit, shat, have shut!
I have loved you both bowl-cut and shagged

There are days when the sun is a great gash
Nights, the moon smokes hashish and falls asleep on your lap

Sorry, but your morphing was not satisfactory
Shapeshifter, you choked on your magic scarf

III.

I heard this joke at the bar
An agnostic dyslexic insomniac stayed up all night searching for doG

The prosperity sign flips right side up again
The Almanac says this Ox Year we'll toil like good immigrants

Horse is frigid. Mule can't love
Salmon dead at the redd

One leg is stationary, the other must tread, must tread, must tread
The Triads riddled him, then us

What is the heart's past participle?
She would have loved not to have loved

I bought you at the corner of *Agave* and *Revolucíon*
You wrapped yourself thrice around my green arm and shat!

A childless woman can feel the end of all existence
Look, on that bloody spot, Chrysanthemum!

Shamanka, fetch your grandmother at the bus stop
Changeling, you are the one I love

Tonight while the Stars Are Shimmering
(New World Duet)

A burst of red hibiscus on the hill
> A dahlia-blue silence chills the path

Compassion falters on highway 8
> Between La Jolla and Julian you are sad

Across the Del Mar shores I ponder my dead mother
> Between heaven and earth, a pesky brown gull

The sky is green where it meets the ocean
> You're the master of subterfuge, my love

A plume of foul orange from a duster plane
> I wonder what poison he is releasing, you say

A steep wall of wildflowers, perhaps verbena
> Purple so bright they mock the robes of God

In Feudal China you would've been drowned at birth
> In India charred for a better dowry

How was I saved on that boat of freedom
> To be anointed here on the prayer mat of your love?

High humidity, humiliation on the terrain
> Oi, you can't describe the ocean to the well frog

I call you racist, you call me racist
> Now, we're entering forbidden territory

I call you sexist, you call me a fool
> And compare the canyons to breasts, anyway

I pull your hair, you bite my nape

                  We make mad love until birdsong morning

You tear off your shirt, you cry out to the moon

                  In the avocado grove you find peaches

You curse on the precipice, I weep near the sea

            The *Tribune* says NOBODY WILL MARRY YOU
YOU'RE ALREADY FORTY

               My mother followed a cockcrow, my granny a dog

Their palms arranged my destiny

                Look, there's Orion, look, the Dog Star

Sorry, your majesty, your poetry has lost its *duende*

                  Look, baby, baby, stop the car

A mouse and a kitty hawk, they are dancing

Yellow-mauve marguerites close their faces at dusk

                Behind the iron gate, a jasmine breeze

In life we share a pink quilt, in death a blue vault

             Shall we cease this redress, this wasteful ransom?

Your coffee is bitter, your spaghetti is sad

              Is there no ending this colloquy?

Ms. Lookeast, Ms. Lookeast

            What have we accomplished this century?

I take your olive branch deep within me

                              A white man's guilt, a white man's love
Tonight while the stars are shimmering

Bad Date Polytich, Eight Poems

BAD DATE

I won't say where I went to dinner,
　　Because my host is a Sado-Scorpio.
He served me Perfume River Ratatouille
　　From Mrs. Min's Village Wok video.

He pretended to be well-meaning.
　　His décor flaunted *multicultural*—
Two shriveled heads from Borneo,
　　A cornice from a temple in Kyoto,
Red Mansion sex pics on tusks,
　　Hirohito's mangled sword on the mantle.

He squeezed my knee with gusto,
　　Then, invited me back for tomorrow.

Family Restaurant (#1)

Empty Lotus Room, no patrons
  Only a telephone rings and rings
Muffled by an adjoining wall
  He murmurs to a distant lover
His wife head-bent peeling shrimp
  Hums an ancient tune about magpies
His daughter wide-eyed, little fists
  Vows to never forgive him
His shadow enters the deep forest
  Blackening the shimmering moss

Family Restaurant (#2)

The old neon flickers and hums.
The grandmother turns it off.
The boy empties the last of the trash,
Eager to return to the prom.
The grandmother gestures him back,
Fan loy, fan loy, waving both arms.
He curses *Goddam old hag,*
Rolls up his tux sleeves gingerly,
Sorts out the bones from the glass.

Empathy
for Janie

I was in line for rice gruel
You were in line for bread
When I returned for another dollop
I saw a giant ringworm gnawing your head

You were shaved immediately
"Feels much better" you said
But I was the child left scratching
Scratching until I bled.

Blues on Yellow (#3)

No time to cry   no time to dwell
Forgive the butchers of Nanking   forgive past pogroms
Get out   get out   of your shell
You're not the century's last orphan
Unmat your hair   red-lacquer your fingernails
Douse your pussy with lavender
Cheer up   cheer up   dress up   to kill
A dingy yellow wallflower   not   comely
There's no decorum in happiness
He'll bury his wan love   deep into your well

FOLK SONG REVISITED
(to the tune of "Her Door Opens to White Waters")

My friend Mieko Ono bought a condo
Over a brand-new wooden footbridge
In Miami University, Oxford, Ohio
She teaches Japanese to Business Minors
Each night she dims the stone lanterns
She lives there alone without a lover

Ohio/Ohio
for Mieko

There is a spot near your broken heart
        Stupid pupils, they're blind
You teach them the Kanji for love
          The tenth stroke is the great aorta
Only one girl saw your terror

Ten thousand in this village, but you're unloved
        Breasts should be kissed
Not lopped
        A cold bed of chemo awaits
No sister to hold you, no lover

A surgeon's knife is not love
        That which won't kill us will maim us
Fifty, you're still chasing love
        Time's running out, the clock drips regret
Let's cruise the websites for a savior

So, You Fucked John Donne
for MJW

So, you fucked John Donne.
Wasn't very nice of you.
He was betrothed to God, you know,
a diet of worms for you!

So, you fucked John Keats.
He's got the sickness, you know.
You *took precautions*, you say.
So, you fucked him anyway.

John Donne, John Keats,
John Guevara, John Wong,
John Kennedy, Johnny John-John.
The beautiful, the wreckless, the strong.

Poor thang, you had no self-worth then,
you fucked them all for a song.

Identity Poem (#99)

Are you the sky—or the allegory for loneliness?
Are you the only Chinese restaurant in Roseburg, Oregon?
A half-breed war orphan—adopted by proper Christians?

A heathen poidog, a creamy half-and-half?
Are you a dingy vinyl address book? A wrist
Without a corsage? Are you baby's breath

Faced down on a teenage road in America?
Are you earphones—detached
Left dangling on an airplane jack to diaspora?

Are you doomed to a childhood without music?
Weary of your granny's one-string, woe-be-gone *erhu*
Mewling about the past

Are you hate speech or are you a lullaby?
Anecdotes requiring footnotes
An ethnic joke rehashed

How many Chinamen does it take—to screw
How many Chinamen does it take—to screw
A lightbulb?

Are you so poor that you cannot call your mother?
You have less than two dollars on your phonecard
And it's a long cable to Nirvana

Are you a skylight through which the busgirl sees heaven?
A chopping block stained by the blood of ten thousand innocents
Which daily, the same busgirl must wipe off

Does existence preempt essence?
I "being" what my ancestors were not
Suddenly, you're a vegan vegetarian!

Restaurant is a facticity and
Getting the hell out—is transcendence
Was the punch line "incandescent"?

Was a nosebleed your last tender memory of her?
Did he say no dogs and Chinawomen?
Are you a rose—or a tattoo of fire?

To Pursue the Limitless

To pursue the limitless
With a hare-brained paramour
To chase a dull husband
With a sharp knife

To speak to Rose
About her thorny sisters
Lock the door behind you
The restaurant is on fire

You are named after
Flower and precious metal
You are touched
By mercury

Your birth-name is Dawning
Your milk-name is Twilight
Your betrothed name is Dusk

To speak in dainty aphorisms
To dither
In monosyllables
Binomes copulating in midair

To teach English as a second
Third, fourth language

You were faithful to the original
You were married to the Chinese paradox

美言不信　信言不美

Beautiful words are not truthful
The truth is not beautiful

You have translated "bitter" as "melon"
"Fruit" as "willful absence"

You were mum as an egg
He was brutal as an embryo
Blood-soup will congeal in the refrigerator

You are both naturalized citizens
You have the right to a little ecstasy

To (二) err is human
To (五) woo is woman

Mái mā   Buried mother
Mài mía   Sold hemp
Mǎi mā   Bought horse
No, not the tones but the tomes

You said *My name is Zhuang Mei*
    Sturdy Beauty
But he thought you said *Shuang Mei*
    Frosty Plum

He brandished his arc of black hair like a coxcomb
He said *Meet me at the airport travelator*
His back door was lovelier than his front door

A smear of bile on your dress
Proved his existence

Summer Sonatina

You turn your head and I shall never see you again,
My youth, my summer, lorries passing.

Damask roses, Vivaldi's 4th season, clichéd and beautiful.
My tongue is glib, I shall tangle the strings of your heart.
My version of history: palanquins, wrists, the red descent of peonies.
Enter the turtle, my mother's back, take what you desire.
What do I have to lose, sweet immigrant, but everything.

———

That tintype you embraced, was it not of your father?
That dagguerotype you erased, was it not of your mother?
The opera you lampooned, was it not *The Jade Hairpin*?
The phoenix broken, her emerald eyes dangle.

You must not sing praise on the same day of mourning.
You must serve the mind and the "doctrine of the mean."
You must learn to chant the names of birds & beasts & flowers.

———

Yellow Pearl, I bemoan your preciousness.
They will pluck you from the great chancre.
The soft palette lolls, not quite bilingual.

Don't tell them, says mother, they will deport you.
Don't tell them, says father, I was a paperson.
Don't tell them, says brother, our misery is our own.

Kingdoms come, kingdoms go, but family is forever.

———————

You were splayed on a Cal-Rose sticky-rice bag with a waiter named
    Damien.
Your hair black as raven, his——blond as rope.
I thought you were dead, but you were tired from pleasure.
But sister, we're not supposed to feel until we've passed the Bar Exam.
We must not sully our frock behind the pantry, sedge and mallow.

———————

He is so fair you can see the Thames pulsing in his temples.
So fair, he blanched the skies of the suburbs.
You love him anyway, his beauty is all you know.
So fair, you imagine sowing his gray children.
In a parking lot, you say to Marguerite,
"Why must I yearn for his bland porridge?"

We search for the Great Elixir,
                    manless, childless,
Without a cloud in the sky.

—————

Thank you for your graciousness, a pair of porcelain nags,
    Yo-Yo Ma's lugubrious cello.
Thank you for the CDs of Prince, Ravel and The Time,
    for the Cornish game hens at Yaddo.

—————

Necks, gizzards, livers—tucked in the cervix.
Dark meat, white meat, you prefer the white.
Plucked, dressed, they look like important composers.
When you clean the head, don't forget the eyes.
The soft palette behind the cheeks, extra tender.
The scales scraped backward crackle like ice,
Tiny shattered pupils, we can see our reflections.

—————

Some American poet said to me, *The Haiku is dead.*
    I thought, *pink and swollen, something sad about his body.*

He said, *The Tao is untranslatable and the Haiku is dead.*
    I thought, *pink and swollen, something sad about his body.*

The poet guards the conscience of society—no, you're wrong.
She stands lonely on that hillock observing the pastures.
The world scoffs back with bog and terror.
Fake paradise, imported palmettos,
O Prince, do not lose your soul in the ramparts.
West of Chin's edge, there are no new friends.

Horseyear

for Jane Cooper

In the margins you roam free
As far as the paddock will take you
The poet has lost her chariot
Stumbling for the orchard in twilight

Your Toyota's stuck in the mud
Push, push 100 pound girl
Already you're a millennium late
Your forelock soaked in rain

Who will take that bit?
Your mouth is hard or tender?
Your flesh is deep in your sheath
Who is holding the tether?

The bones of the dead are fragrant
They breathe in lush desire
Joss ticks and peonies ablaze
To secure their eternal fame

When young you learned the flute
When old you taught the zither
Forty, you wrote for love
Seventy, you yearn for God

The eyes of Kuanyin can't lie
A tear shall fall from heaven
She brought us here on her back
America, our legs are broken

Hack a river in his thigh
Augur from the skull of our beloved
Kiss his bract of hemlock
Hardened in river clay

His soul has been dead for years
His body's flexion bronze
A midvein pulses blue
The killing floor glistens

Bosnia, a headless wound
Los Angeles, a blistering glans
Rwanda, a whither of blood
The killing floor glistens

Our yokes and goads are broken
Wheel locks in idle wind
We love you from a distant wasteland
Our prayer the blackdrop of sky

————

 We sit alone with our porridge
Whose name is Budget Gourmet
We've missed our chance in love
O brief and fallen Orchid

Beautiful, cut-sliced moon
O muse of X-Acto knife and rain
Cocked between dream and window frame
O pale and loitering suitor

Climb the liana of the mansion
Begging bowl in hand
We hunger for love and fame
A piece of the world at sunset

Our pupils will avenge our deaths
Our rivals will fall to disgrace
Jade and gold in their mouths
Plundered over and over

Our hair will grow after death
Our poetry, moss-eaten
Never will we feel fulfilled
Never to reclaim our name

Rhapsody in Plain Yellow

FOR MY LOVE, CHARLES (1938–2000)

Say: 言

I love you, I love you, I love you, no matter
   your race, your sex, your color. Say:
the world is round and the arctic is cold.
   Say: I shall kiss the rondure of your soul's
living marl. Say: he is beautiful,
   serenely beautiful, yet, only ephemerally so.
Say: Her Majesty combs her long black hair for hours.
   Say: O rainbows, in his eyes, rainbows.
Say: O frills and fronds, I know you
   Mr. Snail Consciousness,
O foot plodding the underside of leaves.
   Say: I am nothing without you, nothing,
Ms. Lookeast, Ms. Lookeast,
   without you, I am utterly empty.
Say: the small throat of sorrow.
   Say: China and France, China and France.
Say: Beauty and loss, the dross of centuries.
   Say: Nothing in their feudal antechamber
shall relinquish us of our beauty—
   Say: Mimosa—this is not a marriage song (epithalamion).
Say: when I was a young girl in Hong Kong
   a prince came on a horse, I believe it was piebald.
O dead prince   dead dead prince   who paid for my ardor.

Say: O foot   O ague   O warbling oratorio . . .
Say: Darling, use "love" only as a transitive verb
    for the first forty years of your life.
Say: I have felt this before, it's soft, human.
    Say: my love is a fragile concertina.
Say: you always love them in the beginning,
    then, you take them to slaughter.
O her coarse whispers   O her soft bangs.
    By their withers, they are emblazoned doppelgangers.
Say: beauty and terror, beauty and terror.
    Say: the house is filled with perfume,
dancing sonatinas and pungent flowers.
    Say: houses filled with combs   combs   combs
and the mistress' wan ankles.
    Say: embrace the An Lu Shan ascendancy
and the fantastical diaspora of tears.
    Say: down blue margins
my inky love runs. Tearfully,
    tearfully, the pearl concubine runs.
There is a tear in his left eye—sadness or debris?
    Say: reverence to her, reverence to her.
Say: I am a very small boy, a very small boy,
    I am a teeny weeny little boy
who yearns to be punished.
    Say, I can't live without you

Head Mistress, Head Mistress,

    I am a little lamb, a consenting little lamb,
I am a sheep without his fold.

    Say: God does not exist and hell is other people—
and Mabel, can't we get out of this hotel?

    Say: Gregor Samsa—someone in Tuscaloosa
thinks you're *magnifico,* she will kiss

    your battered cheek, embrace your broken skull.
Is the apple half eaten or half whole?

    Suddenly, he moves within me, how do I know
that he is not death, in death there is

certain // caesura.

Say: there is poetry in his body, poetry

    in his body, yes, say:
this dead love, this dead love,

    this dead, dead love, this lovely death,
this white percale, white of hell, of heavenly shale.

    Centerfolia . . . say: kiss her sweet lips.
Say: what rhymes with "flower":

    "bower," "shower," "power"?
I am that yellow girl, that famished yellow girl

    from the first world.
Say: I don't give a shit about nothing

'xcept my cat, your cock and poetry.
Say: a refuge between sleeping and dying.

Say: to Maui   to Maui   to Maui
creeps in his petty pompadour.

Day to day, her milk of human kindness
ran dry; I shall die of jejune jejune   *la lune la lune.*

Say: a beleaguered soldier, a fine arse had he.
Say: I have seen the small men of my generation
    rabid, discrete, hysterical, lilliput, naked.
Say: Friday is okay; we'll have fish.

Say: Friday is not okay; he shall die
of the measles near the bay.

Say: Friday, just another savage
day until Saturday, the true Sabbath, when they shall
    finally stay.   Say:

                    Sojourner

                        Truth.

Say: I am dismayed by your cloying promiscuousness
    and fawning attitude.
Say: *amaduofu, amaduofu.*

Say: he put cumin and tarragon in his stew.
Say: he's the last wave of French Algerian Jews.

He's a cousin of Helene Cixous, twice removed.
Say: he recites the lost autobiography of Camus.

Say: I am a professor from the University of Stupidity,

I cashed my welfare check and felt good.
     I saw your mama crossing the bridge of magpies
up on the faded hillock with the Lame Ox—
     Your father was conspicuously absent.
Admit that you loved your mother,
     that you killed your father to marry your mother.
Suddenly, my terrible childhood made sense.
     Say: beauty and truth, beauty and truth,
all ye need to know on earth all ye need to know.
     Say: I was boogying down, boogying down
Victoria Peak Way and a slip-of-a-boy climbed off his ox;
     he importuned me for a kiss, a tiny one
on his cankered lip.
     Say: O celebrator   O celebrant
of a blessed life, say:
     false   fleeting   hopes
Say: despair, despair, despair.
     Say: Chinawoman, I am a contradiction in terms:
I embody frugality and ecstasy.
     Friday Wong died on a Tuesday,
O how he loved his lambs.
     He was lost in their sheepfold.
Say: another mai tai before your death.
     Another measure   another murmur   before your last breath.
Another boyfriend, Italianesque.

Say: Save. Exit.

Say: I am the sentence which shall at last elude her.

Oh, the hell of heaven's girth, a low mound from here . . .

Say:

Oh, a mother's vision of the emerald hills draws down her brows.

Say: A brush of jade, a jasper plow furrow.

Say: #####00000xxxxx!!!!

Contemplate   thangs   cerebral   spiritual   open   stuff   reality
  by definition   lack   any   spatial   extension
we occupy   no space   and   are   not   measurable
  we do not move   undulate   are not in   perpetual motion
where   for example   is thinking   in the head?   in my vulva?

  whereas   in my female lack of penis?   Physical
thangs   spatial extensions   mathematically   measurable
  preternaturally   possible   lack bestial   vegetable   consciousness
lack   happiness   lackluster   lack   *chutzpah*   lack   love

Say: A scentless camellia bush bloodied the afternoon.

Fuck this line, can you really believe this?

When did I become the master of suburban bliss?

With whose tongue were we born?

The language of the masters is the language of the aggressors.

We've studied their cadence carefully—

enrolled in a class to *improve our accent.*

   Meanwhile, they hover over, waiting for us to stumble . . .
to drop an article, mispronounce an R.

   Say: softly, softly, the silent gunboats glide.
O onerous sibilants, O onomatopoetic glibness.

   Say:
How could we write poetry in a time like this?

   A discipline that makes much ado about so little?
Willfully laconic, deceptively disguised as a love poem.

Say:
Your engorging dict-
atorial flesh
grazed mine.

Would you have loved me more if I were black?

   Would I have loved you more if you were white?
And you, relentless Sinophile,

   holding my long hair, my frayed dreams.

My turn to objectify you.

   I, the lunatic, the lover, the poet,
the face of an orphan static with flies,

   the scourge of the old world,

which reminds us—it ain't all randy dandy
   in the new kingdom.

Say   rebuke   descry

Hills and canyons, robbed by sun, leave us nothing.

Notes

That Half Is Almost Gone
"That half is almost gone" is a visual play on the Chinese character for
"love": 愛 .
The semantic radical for this character is the character for "heart."
A slash goes straight across the "heart."
"*ai, ai*" is an exclamation homophonous with *ai*/love, punning love
with pain.

The Colonial Language Is English
"The Tao of which we speak is not the eternal Tao
The name that we utter is not the eternal name"
comes from Lao Tzu.

Take a Left at the Waters of Samsara
Samsara: Hindu continous cycle of birth, death and rebirth. This chain
of eternal suffering is a result of karma, accumulated debts from evil
and sinful actions.

Chinese Quatrains
Adapted from *jue-ju*, literally "cut verse," four-lined poems, usually
seven characters per line.

Cauldron
The poem is shaped like a myriad of bronze, three-legged ceremonial

cauldrons (*ding*) one piled on top of another. The final shape should look like one large, abstracted cauldron.

Hong Kong Fathersong
Furama Hotel: an old colonial hotel.
Happy Valley: a racetrack in Hong Kong.
Cat Street: red-light district.
Wanchai: a bustling district in Hong Kong.

Get Rid of the X
The poem is an allusion to a famous lyric by Lipo called "Drinking with the Moon."

How Deep Is the River of God?
"*Guan, guan* cry the ospreys" is an allusion from the *Shih Ching*, an anthology of ancient folk poetry written between 800–600 B.C.

Variations on an Ancient Theme: The Drunken Husband
The dog barking is a conventional opening in many folk songs. The drunken husband is also a conventional character. In this instance, I am alluding to poems in the *Yueh Fu*.

Bold Beauty
Ts'ai Yen (A.D. 200) was a daughter of an important official in the later Han Dynasty. During the Tartar invasion, she was captured and served as wife to the Tartar chief for twelve years. She was finally ransomed and returned to her family. However, her sons were left behind.

The True Story of Mortar and Pestle
The story is derived from a Chinese ghost story in the classical collection *Yuan Hun Chih* (A.D. 550).

Where We Live Now
"Red Detachment of Women" was a Maoist dance drama popular during the cultural revolution.

Tonight while the Stars Are Shimmering
"Between heaven and earth, a pesky brown gull" comes from Tu Fu.
"prayer mat" refers to a classic pornographic novel *The Prayermat of Flesh*.

Family Restaurant (#1)
Inspired by a Wang Wei poem.

Family Restaurant (#2)
"*Fan loy, fan loy*" Cantonese meaning "come back, come back."

Folk Song Revisited
"Her Door Opens to White Waters" is a folk song in the *Yueh Fu*.

Ohio/Ohio
"Ohio" puns with a Japanese greeting.
Kanji: Chinese classical characters absorbed into the Japanese language.
"The tenth stroke . . ." Please refer to the explanation for the character for "love" in the note to "That Half Is Almost Gone" on p. 105.

Identity Poem (#99)
Poidog: American Hawaiian slang for a mongrel, a mixed-race person.

Summer Sonatina

"Kingdoms come, kingdoms go, but family is forever" comes from Confucious.

Rhapsody in Plain Yellow

"Rhapsody" mocks the *fu* form, characterized by long, poetic exposition. An Lu Shan: a famous rebel warrior in the T'ang Dynasty who tried to topple the kingdom.